Paperwell Press

ISBN 978-1-5272-7370-2

Copyright © 2020

Mohammad Ihsan Fazal

With thanks to Anisa and Aminah

The Ultimate "Situational Judgement Test" Revision Guide
A framework for exam success

By Dr Mohammad Ihsân Fazal

Contents

Foreword

This guide seeks to introduce you to the final year UK medical Situational Judgement Test (SJT) exam and its constituent parts. Having excelled in the exam and securing my top job I share my tips and tricks for understanding the context of the SJT and clearly explain a technique which played a big part in my success. This technique will support you in quickly and accurately identifying the correct answer and achieving a high score.

I really do hope you find this useful and best of luck with the exam and your future career!

Introduction

The SJT is an important exam which accounts for 50% of your foundation school application. In other words, it is worth more than every other exam you will sit whilst at medical school. The fact that you are reading this is an indicator that you are taking your preparation seriously, and although the SJT may feel like an arbitrary and, at times, pointless task, I promise you that your revision <u>will</u> make you into a better doctor.

The SJT exposes you to many common ethical and professional scenarios and prepares you to handle them without putting patients or your career at risk. This is an opportunity! You might one day spot an SJT scenario as you walk around hospital, and hopefully your exam preparation will make it easy to act appropriately.

If you are ever feeling demotivated remember that preparing for this exam will give you more confidence in your professional conduct.

Before we begin, I must state this guide assumes you are familiar with the general layout of the test - if you are not, then I suggest you stop here and visit the SJT website. Additionally, you will find some general SJT rules at the end which should prove useful. This guide does not provide questions to practice – the reason why is discussed in 'Revising for the SJT' section.

The SJT tests five specific domains of GMC good medical practice:

1. Commitment to professionalism
2. Coping with pressure
3. Effective communication
4. Patient focus
5. Working effectively as part of a team

It is a good idea to browse the GMC website and glance over the guidance for each domain to familiarise yourself with the general ideas. I advise against memorising the guidelines as the SJT tests your application rather than your recall – also there are quite a lot of guidelines!

The exam is designed to take 140 minutes (2 hours 20 minutes) and is composed of 75 scenarios. In other words, you have 140 minutes to read 75 short paragraphs, ~400

4

options, rank them appropriately and input your answer. Timing is the biggest challenge of this exam and it will be most noticeable during the actual paper which is why preparing and familiarising yourself with the exam format is so important. It is wise to familiarise yourself with the online demo (available from the Pearson Vue website) so there are no surprises on the day of the exam.

The exam is split into three sections:

- Part A: Rating (18 scenarios)
- Part B: Multiple choice (20 scenarios)
- Part C: Ranking (37 scenarios).

In Part A (scenarios 1 to 18) you will be faced with a scenario and between 4 to 8 questions with responses which you must rate. Each response appears on its own page with the scenario and four options. The options vary depending on the response format. If the response format is an action or a verbal statement you will be asked to select how appropriate that action or statement is (inappropriate, somewhat inappropriate, somewhat appropriate, very appropriate). If the response is a consideration e.g. you want to leave on time today, you will be asked to select how important that consideration is [not at all important, of minor importance, important, very important]. An important thing that you must keep in mind when tackling Part A is that the questions are totally independent from each other. When deciding how appropriate an action is, consider it in isolation and do not be influenced by your previous answer.

6

In Part B (scenarios 18 to 38), you will be presented with a scenario and asked to select the three most appropriate options from a list of eight. As before, these can be actions, considerations, or verbal statements. There is an important distinction here which sets this section apart from the others. The choices you make in Part B must make sense together and the appropriateness of your choices is judged together. This is the key to tackling Part B questions. If you are ever stuck, look at the options you have chosen they should make sense chronologically and without contradiction. If not, then you have made a mistake!

In Part C of the paper (questions 39 to 75), you will be presented with a scenario and asked to rank five options from the most appropriate to least appropriate using a drag-and-drop interface. As before, these can be actions, considerations, or verbal statements. This part makes up the bulk of the exam in terms of time and mental energy required. Additionally, it is the classic SJT question style from which the others are derived and for which there is the most official material available for revision. I will discuss this in depth later in this guide.

SJT Marking

I will now explore the SJT marking process, so you have a better appreciation for why your answer selection (and thorough preparation) is important. In Part B, you will score marks for correct answers with each incorrect answer scoring 0. For the rating (part A) and ranking (part B) questions, points are distributed using a more confusing method referred to as 'near miss'.

Using the example of a question where the correct ranking is EBDAC, points would be allocated as follows:

	Your answer				
Correct order	Rank 1	Rank 2	Rank 3	Rank 4	Rank 5
E	4	3	2	1	0
B	3	4	3	2	1
D	2	3	4	3	2
A	1	2	3	4	3
C	0	1	2	3	4

So, if your ranking perfectly matches the correct order, each answer gets 4 points giving a total of 20 marks. You lose a point for every position you have deviated from the correct rank. Using the above example, an answer of CBDAE would yield 12 marks – ranking the correct top choice as bottom (0 points) and the correct bottom choice as top (0 points) and with the other 3 in the correct place (3 x 4 points). A similar process applies to Part A rating questions. The distance of your choice from the correct answer dictates the mark received. From this you can appreciate you are penalised most heavily for ranking the most appropriate option as the least appropriate.

Revising for the SJT

With the digital format of the exam, you may feel apprehensive about how to revise especially considering the disconnect between the official SJT mock papers and the demo exam available on the Pearson Vue website. However, do not be thrown off by the new format and the addition of the new section. Think of Part A as a spread-out Part C, it is testing the same knowledge and thought process that you go through when faced by a Part C question.

Now that I have reassured you somewhat (I hope!), I will put forward the thesis of this guide and the process that should help you to score highly. Taking Part A and C questions as an example, generally, in each question it is quite clear which answer should be in the top spot and which should be at the bottom. To excel you need the middle three to be correct and these are often much less obvious. Your answer must match the nuanced judgement of the SJT. Using question banks is not advisable, as they will be based on the author's own thought process rather than that of the SJT. By using question banks, you risk influencing your judgement in a way that will not benefit your exam performance.

Understanding that the SJT scenarios occur in a magic SJT world with its own SJT rules gives you an angle of attack. If you can identify and learn these rules, you can apply them to any situation that the exam throws your way and score better. I will outline an approach to revision and a process for you to achieve this.

The aim is to identify where your judgements conflict with the SJT world and to create a generic framework derived from official exam material to support your future decision making.

General approach

The SJT is not an exam that requires several months of preparation. Working most evenings for a month should be sufficient, however, the more preparation the better. I suggest you use your time as follows with whatever intensity you see fit:

1. Attempt mock paper 1

2. Mark mock paper 1

3. Attempt mock paper 2

4. Mark mock paper 2

5. Re-attempt mock paper 1

6. Compare both marked answers of mock paper 1

7. **Identify weakness**

8. **Generalise rationale**

9. Repeat for mock paper 2

10. Repeat cycle ad nauseum

11. When you tire of this, generalise your correct answers

Identify weakness

To do well in the SJT you need to identify any weakness in your own judgement. By this, I mean after completing a paper twice compare the answers of the two attempts side by side. The logic is if you were incorrect in the first attempt, you should not make the same mistake again, as you have already seen the answer. If you have repeated the error this suggests a weakness in your situational judgment. This is by no means an exact science so if you feel your errors were due to inattention that is fine, however, I encourage you to be strict on yourself. Go through the paper and highlight the questions you have repeatedly answered incorrectly so you can begin to address the bias in your judgement. I refer to this process of correction as 'generalisation'.

Generalisation

Generalisation is a simple concept where you re-write the question stem and the possible answers using generalised language. This will create a framework personal to you which you can apply to any similar situation and will help you to identify patterns specific to the SJT way

of thinking. Use simple language you are

comfortable with to spare your mental energy –

this is especially significant during more intense

revision sessions.

I will now go through and discuss an example of

generalisation.

After completing a mock exam twice and identifying a repeat error we will focus on the question stem. The aim here is to try and identify the general features of the situation. For example, the stem may read:

"At FY1 teaching the Infection Control Team informs everyone that hospital staff should be bare below the elbows. While working, you notice that your FY1 colleague is always wearing his Rolex wristwatch."

Here we can identify the general theme as being **you see your F1 colleague doing something wrong**. This is our generalised scenario. The language should be precise – 'F1 colleague' not just 'colleague' as understandably situations involving nurses or seniors will probably require different actions – e.g. we cannot report our consultant to our consultant.

Once we have tackled the scenario, we must now do the same with the choices. We will take the example of the following possible answers – before we continue, have a go at ranking them:

- **Talk to your FY1 colleague**
- **Discuss your observation with your registrar**
- **Discuss what you have seen with the nurse in charge of the ward**
- **Do not raise your concern immediately. Keep an eye on your colleague over the next few days.**
- **Inform infection control that your FY1 colleague is in breach of policy**

18

Spoiler alert

They are already in the correct order.

We can identify the general themes in the choices as follows:

- **Approach FY1 colleague directly**
- **Escalate to senior**
- **Escalate to non-direct senior**
- **Do nothing / Wait and see**
- **Escalate to the extreme**

By simplifying the language, we have made it much easier to identify which is most appropriate. Additionally, by converting the question into a generic scenario we can now easily apply it to another situation - for example, in the real SJT if a question stated:

19

You see your FY1 colleague drinking alcohol on the ward.

We have successfully built a framework that we know is based on SJT principles and is ready to be applied in the exam. With this framework in hand, you can choose to commit it to memory or simply familiarise yourself with it. Either way you have an advantage over someone who has aimlessly attempted the mocks or completed loads of question banks.

Framework examples

In the following pages you will find examples of generalised SJT scenarios for each domain along with their generalised answers in the correct order.

Professionalism

Lack of learning opportunities

1. Talk to senior
2. Help colleagues on another ward
3. Escalate (e.g. to foundation programme lead)
4. Stop work / change job
5. Not addressing issue

Colleague abusing patient / being unprofessional

1. Approach colleague directly

2. Escalate appropriately (colleague's line manager)

3. Investigate the situation

4. Escalate to the extreme (call Head of Deanery etc)

5. Do nothing

Dealing with blood test / treatment error

1. Immediate intervention

2. Escalate appropriately

3. Consult another F1

4. Correct retrospectively (e.g. make an entry in notes stating correction)

5. Leave it to someone else

Is anyone here a doctor? / medical assistance needed in public place

1. Intervene immediately but make your limitations known
2. Ask people present to find someone more senior
3. Do not respond but have a look and see if you can help
4. Wait and see if anyone else steps up
5. Do nothing

Accepting gifts from patients

1. Tell patient politely that you cannot accept a gift
2. Escalate and ask a senior
3. Suggest patient donates to charity
4. Explore their reason for giving a gift
5. Ask for more

Coping with pressure

Asked to consent patient for procedure

1. Colleague doing treatment should consent

2. Do colleague's other tasks so they are available to consent

3. Get another appropriately qualified staff to consent

4. Consent but involve an unqualified colleague (e.g. nurse)

5. Consent the patient yourself

Colleague thinks you have a mental health issue (e.g. depression, burnout)

1. Immediate intervention

2. See your GP (implies a delay)

3. Talk to senior (may not be psych trained so benefit is limited)

4. Talk to fellow F1

5. Self-medicate / treat yourself

Patient you do not know asks a specific question about their care

1. Stall them and find out the plan yourself

2. Offer to ask senior to come and talk to them

3. Tell them that the nurse can answer their question

4. Research / learn about the topic

5. Give an answer you are not sure about

Senior offers to help you out (e.g. sign you off for a skill)

1. Ask senior to formally assess you

2. Ask senior to sign for what they have seen you do (but not formally assessed)

3. Report them to clinical supervisor

4. Let them help you and tell other F1s they are easy to get signoffs from.

5. Threaten to escalate if they do not sign more

Communication

Patient wants to start / stop / change treatment but does not want family to know (e.g. patient wanting to stop chemo)

1. Listen and respond honestly

2. Discuss with MDT

3. Discuss with GP

4. Break confidentiality and tell family

5. Go against patient wishes

Relative wants an update on a patient's treatment – you do not know the patient

1. Check if relative is next of kin / get consent

2. Ask a colleague who knows the patient to update relative

3. Ask relative to call back later when patient's doctor is back

4. Tell relative you cannot update them

5. Ask nurse to tell relative there is no doctor available to talk

Colleague feels your communication has made patient / relative upset

1. Directly address patient / relative concerns

2. Ask colleague to explore patient / relative concerns

3. Ask colleague why she feels that way

4. Involve a senior

5. Hand over to evening team

Patient focus

Patient needs urgent referral but your SHO says the service is too busy so do it tomorrow

1. Explain why the referral is needed

2. Talk to senior

3. Delegate referral to a nurse

4. Make referral last job of the day

5. Follow instruction and refer tomorrow

Your friend / family is in hospital and asks fc special treatment

1. Explore their concerns

2. Refuse politely as it is inappropriate

3. Ask senior if it is ok

4. Report your friend to security / ward

5. Punish your friend by doing the opposite of what they asked

You notice your patient has been given the wrong treatment

1. Check if the treatment has been given

2. Tell ward manager immediately

3. Tell patient they have received wrong treatment

4. Complete incident form then tell patient

5. Write incident in notes and do not tell patient.

Working effectively as part of a team

Colleague says they have a chronic physical disease

1. Explore how they feel

2. Advise them to see education supervisor

3. Keep an eye on them

4. Advise them to get counselling

5. Tell the consultant

You overhear that an F1 has done something illegal and is not going to report it

1. Approach them directly

2. See their educational supervisor

3. Tell them you are going to report them to

   the GMC

4. Investigate what happened

5. Do nothing

Senior sometimes seems to be not fit to work

1. Approach directly

2. Contact medical defence organisation

3. Discuss with educational supervisor

4. Discuss with F1 colleague

5. Discuss with multiple people from different professions

Part B Questions

My advice for preparing for these types of questions is to focus on the frameworks. These will guide you as to which are the better options. Again, bear in mind that all the three choices must make sense in combination and are normally in chronological order e.g. reach for a glass of water, pick it up, drink it. Having that firmly lodged in your mind should make these questions straightforward.

Comments and general rules

Developing a framework for a scenario or set of scenarios gives us a better understanding of what the SJT world values, but we can develop this further. By analysing the order of the choices in the framework we can extract rules of the SJT world. Taking our initial framework example:

You see your F1 colleague doing something wrong

- **Approach FY1 colleague directly**
- **Escalate to senior**
- **Escalate to non-direct senior**
- **Do nothing / Wait and see**
- **Escalate to the extreme**

34

Focus on any options which may not be immediately clear to you and write out a one sentence rule. For example, **escalating to non-direct senior is better than doing nothing**. This may seem obvious but after doing 50 scenarios under time pressure you may find your mind is not working as well as you would like. Having a personal list of these rules will give you more information of the SJT world and will allow you to make assumptions comfortable in the knowledge that they are reflective of the SJT world. This will contribute to your overall performance as you will spend less time agonising over whether your choices are correct.

I will pause here to give you some general rules of the SJT world. Please use this as a starting point to guide your own list generation.

- The SJT tests what you SHOULD do not what you WOULD do or what you see happen in real life.

- The SJT takes place in the ideal world.

- If you have a concern / problem with a colleague, approaching them directly is nearly always the best option.

- The choice that involves immediate intervention is normally first place with a choice involving delayed action being lower in the list.

- A choice that involves doing nothing is normally one place above doing something totally wrong / inappropriate.

- The patient is more important than you or your colleagues unless this involves exhaustion on your part (which would endanger other patients).

- GP and clinic appointments have minimal waiting times.

- Referrals are readily accepted.

- A senior is always available so breaking bad news is not your job.

- An FY1's role is decision making under guidance so if there is any uncertainty or family is involved consult a senior.

- If a senior has made a plan, it is not your place to modify it (even if you have the knowledge to do so).

- If someone is in your team then they are familiar with the patient.

- Do not transfer responsibility of a patient to another doctor via a nurse.

- Do not prioritise an unknown over a known (e.g. leaving a sick patient because another patient might be sick).

- If your colleague witnessed something it is their responsibility to deal with it not yours.

- If a colleague is performing poorly do not offer to do their work for them, this reinforces bad practice.

- With regards to confidentiality, best to worst answers rely on leaking the least amount of patient information.

- "Complaining" means not trying to resolve the issue and not working collaboratively with others.

- Asking someone if they have the patient's permission to discuss personal information is not sufficient – they may be lying.

- If there is an organisational problem (e.g. nurses are busy) rather than an emergency, you should not have to stay late.

- Having a discussion with the patient about their concerns is better than reassuring them.

- Writing something down, even if you tell the recipient face-to-face that you will write it down, is not as good as telling them the information or handing it over to an appropriately qualified colleague.

- Where possible, give your colleagues an opportunity to rectify / defend themselves (e.g. confront someone directly)

- Sex between an under 13-year-old and an over 13-year-old is illegal.

- In under 13s, it is rarely appropriate for them to consent for treatment without parental involvement.

- If a 16 to 17-year-old refuses treatment you can act in best interests if treatment is avoiding serious harm.

- You cannot delay certifying death until the next day.

Parting words

You can prepare for the SJT. It is not the 'random number generator' that people make it out to be. It is a very time pressured exam so always try to practice under timed conditions. If you put the work in, you will find the SJT helps you to be a better doctor and that should be your focus. Be the best doctor you can be to help the most people in the best way that you can. I hope you have found this guide useful.

Printed in Great Britain
by Amazon